Who Moved My Cheese?

is being used by men and women in many corporations, governmental agencies, the military, small businesses, hospitals, churches and schools, including:

AAA • Amway • Anheuser Busch • Apple Computers • AT&T • Avis • Bausch & Lomb • Bell South • B F Goodrich • Bristol Myers Squibb • Blue Cross • Budget • Cigna • Chase Manhattan • Citibank • 3 Com • Compaq • Dell Computers • Exxon • Federal Health Care Financing Agency • First Union • Franklin Mint • General Motors • Georgia Pacific • Goodyear • Greyhound • GTE Directories • Hewlett-Packard • Home Savings • Hartford Insurance • IBM • Kodak • Lockheed Martin • Lucent Technologies • Marriott • MCI • Mead Johnson • Mercedes Benz • Merck • Mobil • Morgan Stanley • Nations Bank • NCAA • Nestle • Nordstrom • NY Stock Exchange • Oceaneering • Ohio State University • Pepsi • Pitney Bowes • Procter & Gamble • Pep-Boys • Pillsbury • Sara Lee • Shell • Smith Kline Beecham • SouthWest Airlines • Texaco • Time Warner • Health Care • US Army, Navy & Airforce • Whirlpool • Xerox

WHO MOVED MY CHEESE?

"Every once in a while a book comes along that opens a door to the future. This book has had that effect on me."

—David A. Heenan, Board Member
PETER F. DRUCKER MANAGEMENT CENTER

"As soon as I finished reading this, I ordered copies to help us deal with the relentless changes we face—from being on changing teams to developing new markets."

—Joan Banks, Performance Effectiveness Specialist
WHIRLPOOL CORPORATION

"I can picture myself reading this wonderful story to my children and grandchildren in our family room with a warm fire glowing, and their understanding the lessons."

—Lt. Col. Wayne Washer
AERONAUTICAL SCIENCE CENTER, PATTERSON AFB

"Dr. Johnson's enticing images and language give us a fundamentally sound and memorable way of managing change."

—Albert J. Simone, President
ROCHESTER INSTITUTE OF TECHNOLOGY

Books by Spencer Johnson, M.D.

THE ONE MINUTE MANAGER®
(with Kenneth Blanchard, Ph.D.)

THE PRECIOUS PRESENT: The Gift That Makes You
Happy Forever

THE ONE MINUTE $ALES PERSON (with Larry Wilson)

THE ONE MINUTE MOTHER

THE ONE MINUTE FATHER

THE ONE MINUTE TEACHER
(with Constance Johnson, M.Ed.)

ONE MINUTE FOR YOURSELF
(formerly ONE MINUTE FOR MYSELF)

"YES" OR "NO": The Guide to Better Decisions

THE VALUETALES® SERIES FOR CHILDREN

Who Moved My Cheese?

An A-Mazing Way To Deal With Change
In Your Work And In Your Life

WITHDRAWN

Spencer Johnson

Large Print Edition

G. P. PUTNAM'S SONS
NEW YORK

Dedicated to my friend
Dr. Kenneth Blanchard,
whose enthusiasm for this story
encouraged me to write this book,
and whose help brought it to so many people.

G. P. Putnam's Sons
Publishers Since 1838
a member of
Penguin Putnam Inc.
375 Hudson Street
New York, NY 10014

The text of this Large Print edition is unabridged.
Other aspects of the book may vary from the original edition.

Library of Congress Cataloging-in-Publication Data

Johnson, Spencer.
Who moved my cheese? : an a-mazing way to deal with change
in your work and in your life / Spencer Johnson.
p.   cm.
ISBN 0-399-14446-3
1. Change (Psychology)   I. Title.
BF637.C4J64   1998   98-15502 CIP
155.2'4—dc21

(Large Print Edition) ISBN 0-399-14724-1

Printed in the United States of America
1 2 3 4 5 6 7 8 9 10

This book is printed on acid-free paper. ∞
Book design by Masaaki Marler

This Large Print Edition published in accord with the standards of NAVH.

The best laid schemes
o' mice and men
often go astray

Robert Burns
1759–1796

———————

"Life is no straight and easy corridor along
which we travel free and unhampered,
but a maze of passages,
through which we must seek our way,
lost and confused, now and again
checked in a blind alley.

But always, if we have faith,
a door will open for us,
not perhaps one that we ourselves
would ever have thought of,
but one that will ultimately
prove good for us."

A. J. Cronin

Who Moved My Cheese?

CONTENTS

Parts of All of Us 10

The Story Behind The Story
by Kenneth Blanchard, Ph.D. 11

A Gathering: Chicago. 19

The Story of Who Moved My Cheese? 23
Four Characters
Finding Cheese
No Cheese!
The Mice: Sniff & Scurry
The Littlepeople: Hem & Haw
Meanwhile, Back In The Maze
Getting Beyond Fear
Enjoying The Adventure
Moving With The Cheese
The Handwriting On The Wall
Tasting New Cheese
Enjoying Change!

A Discussion: Later That Same Day 75

Share It With Others 93
About The Author 95

PARTS OF ALL OF US

The Simple and The Complex

The four imaginary characters
depicted in this story—
the mice: "Sniff" and "Scurry," and
the littlepeople: "Hem" and "Haw"—
are intended to represent the simple and
the complex parts of ourselves, regardless
of our age, gender, race, or nationality.

Sometimes we may act like
Sniff
Who sniffs out change early, or
Scurry
Who scurries into action, or
Hem
Who denies and resists change as he fears
it will lead to something worse, or
Haw
Who learns to adapt in time when he sees
changing leads to something *better!*

Whatever parts of us we choose to use,
we all share something in common:
a need to find our way in the maze
and succeed in changing times.

The Story Behind The Story
by Kenneth Blanchard, Ph.D.

I am thrilled to be telling you "the story behind the story" of *Who Moved My Cheese?* because it means the book has now been written, and is available for all of us to read, enjoy and share with others.

This is something I've wanted to see happen ever since I first heard Spencer Johnson tell his great "Cheese" story, years ago, before we wrote our book *The One Minute Manager* together.

I remember thinking then how good the story was and how helpful it would be to me from that moment on.

Who Moved My Cheese? is a story about change that takes place in a Maze where four amusing characters look for "Cheese"—cheese being a metaphor for what we want to have in life, whether it is a job, a relationship, money, a big house, freedom, health, recognition, spiritual peace, or even an activity like jogging or golf.

Each of us has our own idea of what Cheese is, and we pursue it because we believe it makes us happy. If we get it, we often become attached to it. And if we lose it, or it's taken away, it can be traumatic.

The "Maze" in the story represents where you spend time looking for what you want. It can be the organization you work in, the community you live in, or the relationships you have in your life.

I tell the Cheese story that you are about to read in my talks around the world, and often hear later from people about what a difference it has made to them.

Believe it or not, this little story has been credited with saving careers, marriages and lives!

One of the many real-life examples comes from Charlie Jones, a well-respected broadcaster for NBC-TV, who revealed that hearing the story of *Who Moved My Cheese?* saved his career. His job as a broadcaster is unique, but the principles he learned can be used by anyone.

Here's what happened: Charlie had worked hard and had done a great job of broadcasting Track and Field events at an earlier Olympic Games, so he was surprised and upset when his boss told him he'd been removed from these showcase events for the next Olympics and assigned to Swimming and Diving.

Not knowing these sports as well, he was frustrated. He felt unappreciated and he became angry. He said he felt it wasn't fair! His anger began to affect everything he did.

Then, he heard the story of *Who Moved My Cheese?*

After that he said he laughed at himself and changed his attitude. He realized his boss had just "moved his Cheese." So he adapted. He learned the two new sports, and in the process, found that doing something new made him feel young.

It wasn't long before his boss recognized his new attitude and energy, and he soon got better assignments. He went on to enjoy more success than ever and was later inducted into Pro Football's Hall of Fame—Broadcasters' Alley.

That's just one of the many real-life stories I've heard about the impact this story has had on people—from their work life to their love life.

I'm such a strong believer in the power of *Who Moved My Cheese?* that I gave a copy of an early pre-publication edition to everyone (more than 200 people) working with our company. Why?

Because like every company that wants to not only survive in the future but stay competitive, The Ken Blanchard Companies are constantly changing. They keep moving our "Cheese." While in the past we may have wanted loyal employees, today we need flexible people who are not possessive about "the way things are done around here."

And yet, as you know, living in constant white water with the changes occurring all the time at work or in life can be stressful, unless people have a way of looking at change that helps them understand it. Enter the *Cheese* story.

When I told people about the story and then they got to read *Who Moved My Cheese?* you could almost feel the release of negative energy beginning to occur. Person after person from every department went out of their way to thank me for the book and told me how helpful it had been to them already in seeing the changes going on in our company in a different light. Believe me, this brief parable takes little time to read but its impact can be profound.

As you turn the pages, you will find three sections in this book. In the first, *A Gathering*, former classmates talk at a class reunion about trying to deal with the changes happening in their lives. The second section is *The Story of Who Moved My Cheese?*, which is the core of the book.

In *The Story* you will see that the two mice do better when they are faced with change because they keep things simple, while the two little-people's complex brains and human emotions complicate things. It is not that mice are smarter. We all know people are more intellegent than mice.

However, as you watch what the four characters do, and realize both the mice and the littlepeople represent parts of ourselves—the simple and the complex—you can see it would be to our advantage to do the simple things that work when things change.

In the third section, *A Discussion,* people discuss what *The Story* meant to them and how they are going to use it in their work and in their lives

Some readers of this book's early manuscript preferred to stop at the end of *The Story*, without reading further, and interpret its meaning for themselves. Others enjoyed reading *A Discussion* that follows because it stimulated their thinking about how they might apply what they'd learned to their own situation.

In any case, I hope each time you re-read *Who Moved My Cheese?* you will find something new and useful in it, as I do, and that it will help you deal with change and bring you success, whatever you decide success is for you.

I hope you enjoy what you discover and I wish you well. Remember: Move with the Cheese!

Ken Blanchard
San Diego, California

Who Moved My Cheese?

A Gathering
Chicago

One sunny Sunday in Chicago, several former classmates, who were good friends in school, gathered for lunch, having attended their high school reunion the night before. They wanted to hear more about what was happening in each other's lives. After a good deal of kidding, and a good meal, they settled into an interesting conversation.

Angela, who had been one of the most popular people in the class, said, "Life sure turned out differently than I thought it would when we were in school. A lot has changed."

"It certainly has," Nathan echoed. They knew he had gone into his family's business, which had operated pretty much the same and had been a part of the local community for as long as they could remember. So, they were surprised when he seemed concerned. He asked, "But, have you noticed how we don't want to change when things change?"

Carlos said, "I guess we resist changing because we're afraid of change."

"Carlos, you were Captain of the football team," Jessica said. "I never thought I'd hear you say anything about being afraid!"

They all laughed as they realized that although they had gone off in different directions—from working at home to managing companies—they were experiencing similar feelings.

Everyone was trying to cope with the unexpected changes that were happening to them in recent years. And most admitted that they did not know a good way to handle them.

Then Michael said, "I used to be afraid of change. When a big change came along in our business, we didn't know what to do. So we didn't adjust and we almost lost it.

"That is," he continued, "until I heard a funny little story that changed everything."

"How so?" Nathan asked.

"Well, the story changed the way I looked at change—from losing something to gaining something—and it showed me how to do it. After that, things quickly improved—at work and in my life.

"At first I was annoyed with the obvious simplicity of the story because it sounded like something we might have been told in school.

"Then I realized I was really annoyed with myself for not seeing the obvious and doing what works when things change.

"When I realized the four characters in the story represented the various parts of myself, I decided who I wanted to act like and I changed.

"Later, I passed the story on to some people in our company and they passed it on to others, and soon our business did much better, because most of us adapted to change better. And like me, many people said it helped them in their personal lives.

"However there were a few people who said they got nothing out of it. They either knew the lessons and were already living them, or, more commonly, they thought they already knew everything and didn't want to learn. They couldn't see why so many others were benefiting from it.

"When one of our senior executives, who was having difficulty adapting, said the story was a waste of his time, other people kidded him saying they knew which character he was in the story—meaning the one who learned nothing new and did not change."

"What's the story?" Angela asked.

"It's called *Who Moved My Cheese?*"

The group laughed. "I think I like it already," Carlos said. "Would you tell us the story? Maybe *we* can get something from it."

"Sure," Michael replied. "I'd be happy to—it doesn't take long." And so he began:

The Story of Who Moved My Cheese?

ONCE, long ago in a land far away, there lived four little characters who ran through a maze looking for cheese to nourish them and make them happy.

Two were mice named "Sniff" and "Scurry" and two were littlepeople—beings who were as small as mice but who looked and acted a lot like people today. Their names were "Hem" and "Haw."

Due to their small size, it would be easy not to notice what the four of them were doing. But if you looked closely enough, you could discover the most amazing things!

Every day the mice and the littlepeople spent time in the maze looking for their own special cheese.

The mice, Sniff and Scurry, possessing only simple rodent brains, but good instincts, searched for the hard nibbling cheese they liked, as mice often do.

The two littlepeople, Hem and Haw, used their brains, filled with many beliefs and emotions, to search for a very different kind of Cheese—with a capital C—which they believed would make them feel happy and successful.

As different as the mice and littlepeople were, they shared something in common: Every morning, they each put on their jogging suits and running shoes, left their little homes, and raced out into the maze looking for their favorite cheese.

The maze was a labyrinth of corridors and chambers, some containing delicious cheese. But there were also dark corners and blind alleys leading nowhere. It was an easy place for anyone to get lost.

However, for those who found their way, the maze held secrets that let them enjoy a better life.

The mice, Sniff and Scurry, used the simple trial-and-error method of finding cheese. They ran down one corridor, and if it proved empty, they turned and ran down another. They remembered the corridors that held no cheese and quickly went into new areas.

Sniff would smell out the general direction of the cheese, using his great nose, and Scurry would race ahead. They got lost, as you might expect, went off in the wrong direction and often bumped into walls. But after a while they found their way.

Like the mice, the two littlepeople, Hem and Haw, also used their ability to think and learn from their past experiences. However, they relied on their complex brains to develop more sophisticated methods of finding Cheese.

Sometimes they did well, but at other times their powerful human beliefs and emotions took over and clouded the way they looked at things. It made life in the maze more complicated and challenging.

Nonetheless, Sniff, Scurry, Hem and Haw all discovered, in their own way, what they were looking for. They each found their own kind of cheese one day at the end of one of the corridors in Cheese Station C.

Every morning after that, the mice and the littlepeople dressed in their running gear and headed over to Cheese Station C. It wasn't long before they each established their own routine.

Sniff and Scurry continued to wake early every day and race through the maze, always following the same route.

When they arrived at their destination, the mice took off their running shoes, tied them together and hung them around their necks—so they could get to them quickly whenever they needed them again. Then they enjoyed the cheese.

In the beginning Hem and Haw also raced toward Cheese Station C every morning to enjoy the tasty new morsels that awaited them.

But after a while, a different routine set in for the littlepeople.

Hem and Haw awoke each day a little later, dressed a little slower, and walked to Cheese Station C. After all, they knew where the Cheese was now and how to get there.

They had no idea where the Cheese came from, or who put it there. They just assumed it would be there.

As soon as Hem and Haw arrived at Cheese Station C each morning, they settled in and made themselves at home. They hung up their jogging suits, put away their running shoes and put on their slippers. They were becoming very comfortable now that they had found the Cheese.

"This is great," Hem said. "There's enough Cheese here to last us forever." The littlepeople felt happy and successful, and thought they were now secure.

It wasn't long before Hem and Haw regarded the Cheese they found at Cheese Station C as *their* cheese. It was such a large store of Cheese that they eventually moved their homes to be closer to it, and built a social life around it.

To make themselves feel more at home, Hem and Haw decorated the walls with sayings and even drew pictures of Cheese around them which made them smile. One read:

Having Cheese
Makes You
Happy.

Sometimes Hem and Haw would take their friends by to see their pile of Cheese at Cheese Station C, and point to it with pride, saying, "Pretty nice Cheese, huh?" Sometimes they shared it with their friends and sometimes they didn't.

"We deserve this Cheese," Hem said. "We certainly had to work long and hard enough to find it." He picked up a nice fresh piece and ate it.

Afterwards, Hem fell asleep, as he often did.

Every night the littlepeople would waddle home, full of Cheese, and every morning they would confidently return for more.

This went on for quite some time.

After a while Hem's and Haw's confidence grew into the arrogance of success. Soon they became so comfortable they didn't even notice what was happening.

As time went on, Sniff and Scurry continued their routine. They arrived early each morning and sniffed and scratched and scurried around Cheese Station C, inspecting the area to see if there had been any changes from the day before. Then they would sit down to nibble on the cheese.

One morning they arrived at Cheese Station C and discovered there was no cheese.

They weren't surprised. Since Sniff and Scurry had noticed the supply of cheese had been getting smaller every day, they were prepared for the inevitable and knew instinctively what to do.

They looked at each other, removed the running shoes they had tied together and hung conveniently around their necks, put them on their feet and laced them up.

The mice did not overanalyze things.

To the mice, the problem and the answer were both simple. The situation at Cheese Station C had changed. So, Sniff and Scurry decided to change.

They both looked out into the maze. Then Sniff lifted his nose, sniffed, and nodded to Scurry, who took off running through the maze, while Sniff followed as fast as he could.

They were quickly off in search of New Cheese.

Later that same day, Hem and Haw arrived at Cheese Station C. They had not been paying attention to the small changes that had been taking place each day, so they took it for granted their Cheese would be there.

They were unprepared for what they found.

"What! No Cheese?" Hem yelled. He continued yelling, "No Cheese? No Cheese?" as though if he shouted loud enough someone would put it back.

"Who moved my Cheese?" he hollered.

Finally, he put his hands on his hips, his face turned red, and he screamed at the top of his voice, "It's not fair!"

Haw just shook his head in disbelief. He, too, had counted on finding Cheese at Cheese Station C. He stood there for a long time, frozen with shock. He was just not ready for this.

Hem was yelling something, but Haw didn't want to hear it. He didn't want to deal with what was facing him, so he just tuned everything out.

The littlepeople's behavior was not very attractive or productive but it was understandable.

Finding Cheese wasn't easy, and it meant a great deal more to the littlepeople than just having enough of it to eat every day.

Finding Cheese was the littlepeople's way of getting what they thought they needed to be happy. They had their own ideas of what Cheese meant to them, depending on their taste.

For some, finding Cheese was having material things. For others it was enjoying good health, or developing a spiritual sense of well-being.

For Haw, Cheese just meant feeling safe, having a loving family someday, and living in a cozy cottage on Cheddar Lane.

To Hem, Cheese was becoming A Big Cheese in charge of others and owning a big house atop Camembert Hill.

Because Cheese was important to them, the two littlepeople spent a long time trying to decide what to do. All they could think of was to keep looking around Cheeseless Station C to see if the Cheese was really gone.

While Sniff and Scurry had quickly moved on, Hem and Haw continued to hem and haw.

They ranted and raved at the injustice of it all. Haw started to get depressed. What would happen if the Cheese wasn't there tomorrow? He had made future plans based on this Cheese.

The littlepeople couldn't believe it. How could this have happened? No one had warned them. It wasn't right. It was not the way things were supposed to be.

Hem and Haw went home that night hungry and discouraged. But before they left, Haw wrote on the wall:

The More Important
Your Cheese Is To You
The More You Want
To Hold On To It.

The next day Hem and Haw left their homes, and returned to Cheese Station C again, where they still expected, somehow, to find *their* Cheese.

The situation hadn't changed; the Cheese was no longer there. The littlepeople didn't know what to do. Hem and Haw just stood there, immobilized like two statues.

Haw shut his eyes as tight as he could and put his hands over his ears. He just wanted to block everything out. He didn't want to know the Cheese supply had gradually been getting smaller. He believed it had been moved all of a sudden.

Hem analyzed the situation over and over and eventually his complicated brain with its huge belief system took hold. "Why did they do this to me?" he demanded. "What's really going on here?"

Finally, Haw opened his eyes, looked around and said, "By the way, where are Sniff and Scurry? Do you think they know something we don't?"

Hem scoffed, "What would they know?"

Hem continued, "They're just simple mice. They just respond to what happens. We're littlepeople. We're smarter than mice. We should be able to figure this out."

"I know we're smarter," Haw said, "but we don't seem to be acting smarter at the moment. Things are changing around here, Hem. Maybe we need to change and do things differently."

"Why should we change?" Hem asked. "We're littlepeople. We're special. This sort of thing should not happen to us. Or if it does, we should at least get some benefits."

"Why should we get benefits?" Haw asked.

"Because we're entitled," Hem claimed.

"Entitled to what?" Haw wanted to know.

"We're entitled to our Cheese."

"Why?" Haw asked.

"Because, we didn't cause this problem," Hem said. "Somebody else did this and we should get something out of it."

Haw suggested, "Maybe we should stop analyzing the situation so much and just get going and find some New Cheese."

"Oh no," Hem argued. "I'm going to get to the bottom of this."

While Hem and Haw were still trying to decide what to do, Sniff and Scurry were already well on their way. They went farther into the maze, up and down corridors, looking for cheese in every Cheese Station they could find.

They didn't think of anything else but finding New Cheese.

They didn't find any for sometime until they finally went into an area of the maze where they had never been before: Cheese Station N.

They squealed with delight. They found what they had been looking for: a great supply of New Cheese.

They could hardly believe their eyes. It was the biggest store of cheese the mice had ever seen.

In the meantime, Hem and Haw were still back in Cheese Station C evaluating their situation. They were now suffering from the effects of having no Cheese. They were becoming frustrated and angry and were blaming each other for the situation they were in.

Now and then Haw thought about his mice friends, Sniff and Scurry, and wondered if they had found any cheese yet. He believed they might be having a hard time, as running through the maze usually involved some uncertainty. But he also knew that it was likely to only last for a while.

Sometimes, Haw would imagine Sniff and Scurry finding New Cheese and enjoying it. He thought about how good it would be for him to be out on an adventure in the maze, and to find fresh New Cheese. He could almost taste it.

The more clearly Haw saw the image of himself finding and enjoying the New Cheese, the more he saw himself leaving Cheese Station C.

"Let's go!" he exclaimed, all of a sudden.

"No," Hem quickly responded. "I like it here. It's comfortable. It's what I know. Besides it's dangerous out there."

"No it isn't," Haw argued. "We've run through many parts of the maze before, and we can do it again."

"I'm getting too old for that," Hem said. "And I'm afraid I'm not interested in getting lost and making a fool of myself. Are you?"

With that, Haw's fear of failing returned and his hope of finding New Cheese faded.

So every day, the littlepeople continued to do what they had done before. They went to Cheese Station C, found no Cheese, and returned home, carrying their worries and frustrations with them.

They tried to deny what was happening, but found it harder to get to sleep, had less energy the next day, and were becoming irritable.

Their homes were not the nurturing places they once were. The littlepeople had difficulty sleeping and were having nightmares about not finding any Cheese.

But Hem and Haw still returned to Cheese Station C and waited there every day.

Hem said, "You know, if we just work harder we'll find that nothing has really changed that much. The Cheese is probably nearby. Maybe they just hid it behind the wall."

The next day, Hem and Haw returned with tools. Hem held the chisel while Haw banged on the hammer until they made a hole in the wall of Cheese Station C. They peered inside but found no Cheese.

They were disappointed but believed they could solve the problem. So they started earlier, stayed longer, and worked harder. But after a while, all they had was a large hole in the wall.

Haw was beginning to realize the difference between activity and productivity.

"Maybe," Hem said, "we should just sit here and see what happens. Sooner or later they have to put the Cheese back."

Haw wanted to believe that. So each day he went home to rest and returned reluctantly with Hem to Cheese Station C. But Cheese never reappeared.

By now the littlepeople were growing weak from hunger and stress. Haw was getting tired of just waiting for their situation to improve. He began to see that the longer they stayed in their Cheeseless situation, the worse off they would be.

Haw knew they were losing their edge.

Finally, one day Haw began laughing at himself. "Haw, haw, look at us. We keep doing the same things over and over again and wonder why things don't get better. If this wasn't so ridiculous, it would be even funnier."

Haw did not like the idea of having to run through the maze again, because he knew he would get lost and have no idea where he would find any Cheese. But he had to laugh at his folly when he saw what his fear was doing to him.

He asked Hem, "Where did we put our running shoes?" It took a long time to find them because they had put everything away when they found their Cheese at Cheese Station C, thinking they wouldn't be needing them anymore.

As Hem saw his friend getting into his running gear, he said, "You're not really going out into the maze again, are you? Why don't you just wait here with me until they put the Cheese back?"

"Because, you just don't get it," Haw said. "I didn't want to see it either, but now I realize they're never going to put yesterday's Cheese back. It's time to find New Cheese."

Hem argued, "But what if there is no Cheese out there? Or even if there is, what if you don't find it?"

"I don't know," Haw said. He had asked himself those same questions too many times and felt the fears again that kept him where he was.

He asked himself. "Where am I more likely to find Cheese—here or in the Maze?"

He painted a picture in his mind. He saw himself venturing out into the Maze with a smile on his face.

While this picture surprised him, it made him feel good. He saw himself getting lost now and then in the Maze, but felt confident he would eventually find New Cheese out there and all the good things that came with it. He gathered his courage.

Then he used his imagination to paint the most believable picture he could—with the most realistic details—of him finding and enjoying the taste of New Cheese.

He saw himself eating Swiss cheese with holes in it, bright orange Cheddar and American cheeses, Italian mozzarella and wonderfully soft French Camembert cheese, and . . .

Then he heard Hem say something and realized they were still at Cheese Station C.

Haw said, "Sometimes, Hem, things change and they are never the same again. This looks like one of those times. That's life! Life moves on. And so should we."

Haw looked at his emaciated companion and tried to talk sense to him, but Hem's fear had turned into anger and he wouldn't listen.

Haw didn't mean to be rude to his friend, but he had to laugh at how silly they both looked.

As Haw prepared to leave, he started to feel more alive, knowing that he was finally able to laugh at himself, let go and move on.

Haw laughed and announced, "It's MAZE time!"

Hem didn't laugh and he didn't respond.

Haw picked up a small, sharp rock and wrote a serious thought on the wall for Hem to think about. As was his custom, Haw even drew a picture of cheese around it, hoping it would help Hem to smile, lighten up, and go after the New Cheese. But Hem didn't want to see it.

It read:

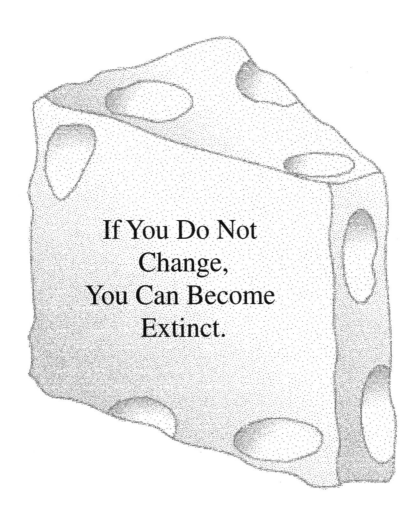

If You Do Not
Change,
You Can Become
Extinct.

Then, Haw stuck his head out and peered anxiously into the maze. He thought about how he'd gotten himself into this cheeseless situation.

He had believed that there may not be any Cheese in the maze, or he may not find it. Such fearful beliefs were immobilizing and killing him.

Haw smiled. He knew Hem was wondering, "Who moved my Cheese?" but Haw was wondering, "Why didn't I get up and move with the Cheese sooner?"

As he started out into the maze, Haw looked back to where he had come from and felt its comfort. He could feel himself being drawn back into familiar territory—even though he hadn't found Cheese there for some time.

Haw became more anxious and wondered if he really wanted to go out into the maze. He wrote a saying on the wall ahead of him and stared at it for some time:

What Would You Do If You Weren't Afraid?

He thought about it.

He knew sometimes some fear can be good. When you are afraid things are going to get worse if you don't do something, it can prompt you into action. But it is not good when you are so afraid that it keeps you from doing anything.

He looked to his right, to the part of the maze where he had never been, and felt the fear.

Then, he took a deep breath, turned right into the maze, and jogged slowly, into the unknown.

As he tried to find his way, Haw worried, at first, that he might have waited too long in Cheese Station C. He hadn't had any Cheese for so long that he was now weak. It took him longer and it was more painful than usual to get through the maze. He decided that if he ever got the chance again, he would get out of his comfort zone and adapt to change sooner. It would make things easier.

Then, Haw smiled a weak smile as he thought, "Better late than never."

During the next several days, Haw found a little Cheese here and there, but nothing that lasted very long. He had hoped to find enough Cheese to take some back to Hem and encourage him to come out into the maze.

But Haw didn't feel confident enough yet. He had to admit, he found it confusing in the maze. Things seemed to have changed since the last time he was out here.

Just when he thought he was getting ahead, he would get lost in the corridors. It seemed his progress was two steps forward and one step backward. It was a challenge, but he had to admit that being back in the maze, hunting for Cheese, wasn't nearly as bad as he feared it might be.

As time went on he began to wonder if it was realistic for him to expect to find New Cheese. He wondered if he had bitten off more than he could chew. Then he laughed, realizing that he had nothing to chew on at the moment.

Whenever he started to get discouraged he reminded himself that what he was doing, as uncomfortable as it was at the moment, was in reality much better than staying in the Cheeseless situation. He was taking control, rather than simply letting things happen to him.

Then he reminded himself, if Sniff and Scurry could move on, so could he!

Later, as Haw looked back on things, he realized that the Cheese at Cheese Station C had not just disappeared overnight, as he had once believed. The amount of Cheese that had been there toward the end had been getting smaller, and what was left had grown old. It didn't taste as good.

Mold may even have begun to grow on the Old Cheese, although he hadn't noticed it. He had to admit however, that if he had wanted to, he probably could have seen what was coming. But he didn't.

Haw now realized that the change probably would not have taken him by surprise if he had been watching what was happening all along and if he had anticipated change. Maybe that's what Sniff and Scurry had been doing.

He decided he would stay more alert from now on. He would expect change to happen and look for it. He would trust his basic instincts to sense when change was going to occur and be ready to adapt to it.

He stopped for a rest and wrote on the wall of the Maze:

Smell The Cheese Often
So You Know
When It Is Getting Old.

Sometime later, after not finding Cheese for what seemed like a long time, Haw finally came across a huge Cheese Station which looked promising. When he went inside, however, he was most disappointed to discover that the Cheese station was empty.

"This empty feeling has happened to me too often," he thought. He felt like giving up.

Haw was losing his physical strength. He knew he was lost and was afraid he would not survive. He thought about turning around and heading back to Cheese Station C. At least, if he made it back, and Hem was still there, Haw wouldn't be alone. Then he asked himself the same question again, "What would I do if I weren't afraid?"

Haw thought he was past his fear, but he was afraid more often than he liked to admit, even to himself. He wasn't always sure what he was afraid of, but, in his weakened condition, he knew now he was simply fearful of going on alone. Haw didn't know it, but he was running behind because he was still weighed down by fearful beliefs.

Haw wondered if Hem had moved on, or if he was still paralyzed by his own fears. Then, Haw remembered the times when he had felt his best in the maze. It was when he was moving along.

He wrote on the wall, knowing it was as much a reminder to himself as it was a marking for his friend Hem, hopefully, to follow:

Movement In A
New Direction
Helps You Find
New Cheese.

Haw looked down the dark passageway and was aware of his fear. What lay ahead? Was it empty? Or worse, were there dangers lurking? He began to imagine all kinds of frightening things that could happen to him. He was scaring himself to death.

Then he laughed at himself. He realized his fears were making things worse. So he did what he would do if he wasn't afraid. He moved in a new direction.

As he started running down the dark corridor he began to smile. Haw didn't realize it yet, but he was discovering what nourished his soul. He was letting go and trusting what lay ahead for him, even though he did not know exactly what it was.

To his surprise, Haw started to enjoy himself more and more. "Why do I feel so good?" he wondered. "I don't have any Cheese and I don't know where I am going."

Before long, he knew why he felt good.

He stopped to write again on the wall:

When You Move
Beyond Your Fear,
You Feel Free.

Haw realized he had been held captive by his own fear. Moving in a new direction had freed him.

Now he felt the cool breeze that was blowing in this part of the maze and it was refreshing. He took in some deep breaths and felt invigorated by the movement. Once he had gotten past his fear, it turned out to be more enjoyable than he once believed it could be.

Haw hadn't felt this way for a long time. He had almost forgotten how much fun it was to go for it.

To make things even better, Haw started to paint a picture in his mind again. He saw himself in great realistic detail, sitting in the middle of a pile of all his favorite cheeses—from Cheddar to Brie! He saw himself eating the many cheeses he liked, and he enjoyed what he saw. Then he imagined how much he would enjoy all their great tastes.

The more clearly he saw the image of himself enjoying New Cheese, the more real and believable it became. He could sense that he was going to find it.

He wrote:

Imagining Myself
Enjoying New Cheese
Even Before I Find It,
Leads Me To It.

Haw kept thinking about what he could gain instead of what he was losing.

He wondered why he had always thought that a change would lead to something worse. Now he realized that change could lead to something better.

"Why didn't I see this before?" he asked himself.

Then he raced through the maze with greater strength and agility. Before long he spotted a Cheese Station and became excited as he noticed little pieces of New Cheese near the entrance.

They were types of Cheeses he had never seen before, but they looked great. He tried them and found that they were delicious. He ate most of the New Cheese bits that were available and put a few in his pocket to have later and perhaps share with Hem. He began to regain his strength.

He entered the Cheese Station with great excitement. But, to his dismay, he found it was empty. Someone had already been there and had left only the few bits of New Cheese.

He realized that if he had moved sooner, he would very likely have found a good deal of New Cheese here.

Haw decided to go back and see if Hem was ready to join him.

As he retraced his steps, he stopped and wrote on the wall:

The Quicker You Let Go
Of Old Cheese,
The Sooner You Find
New Cheese.

After a while Haw made his way back to Cheese Station C and found Hem. He offered Hem bits of New Cheese, but was turned down.

Hem appreciated his friend's gesture but said, "I don't think I would like New Cheese. It's not what I'm used to. I want my *own* Cheese back and I'm not going to change until I get what I want."

Haw just shook his head in disappointment and reluctantly went back out on his own. As he returned to the farthest point he had reached in the maze, he missed his friend, but realized he liked what he was discovering. Even before he found what he hoped would be a great supply of New Cheese, if ever, he knew that what made him happy wasn't just having Cheese.

He was happy when he wasn't being run by his fear. He liked what he was doing now.

Knowing this, Haw didn't feel as weak as he did when he stayed in Cheese Station C with no Cheese. Just realizing he was not letting his fear stop him and knowing that he had taken a new direction nourished him and gave him strength.

Now he felt that it was just a question of time before he found what he needed. In fact, he sensed he had already found what he was looking for.

He smiled as he realized:

It Is Safer To
Search In The Maze
Than Remain In A
Cheeseless Situation.

Haw realized again, as he had once before, that what you are afraid of is never as bad as what you imagine. The fear *you let* build up in your mind is worse than the situation that actually exists.

He'd been so afraid of never finding New Cheese that he didn't even want to start looking. But since starting his journey he had found enough Cheese in the corridors to keep him going. Now he looked forward to finding more. Just looking ahead was becoming exciting.

His old thinking had been clouded by his worries and fears. He used to think about not having enough Cheese, or not having it last as long as he wanted. He used to think more about what could go wrong than what could go right.

But that had changed in the days since he had left Cheese Station C.

He used to believe that Cheese should never be moved and that change wasn't right.

Now he realized it was natural for change to continually occur, whether you expect it or not. Change could surprise you only if you didn't expect it and weren't looking for it.

When he realized he had changed his beliefs, he paused to write on the wall:

Old Beliefs
Do Not Lead You
To New Cheese.

Haw hadn't found Cheese yet, but as he ran through the Maze, he thought about what he had already learned.

Haw now realized that his new beliefs were encouraging new behaviors. He was behaving differently than when he kept returning to the same cheeseless station.

He knew when you change what you believe, you change what you do.

You can believe that a change will harm you and resist it. Or you can believe that finding New Cheese will help you, and embrace the change.

It all depends on what you choose to believe.

He wrote on the wall:

When You See That
You Can Find And
Enjoy New Cheese,
You Change Course.

Haw knew he would be in better shape now if he had dealt with the change much sooner and left Cheese Station C earlier. He would feel stronger in body and spirit and he could have coped better with the challenge of finding New Cheese. In fact, he probably would have found it by now if he had expected change, rather than wasting time denying that the change had already taken place.

He used his imagination again and saw himself finding and savoring New Cheese. He decided to proceed into the more unknown parts of the Maze, and found little bits of Cheese here and there. Haw began to regain his strength and confidence.

As he thought back on where he had come from, Haw was glad he had written on the wall in many places. He trusted that it would serve as a marked trail for Hem to follow through the maze, if he chose to leave Cheese Station C.

Haw just hoped he was heading in the right direction. He thought about the possibility that Hem would read The Handwriting On The Wall and find his way.

He wrote on the wall what he had been thinking about for some time:

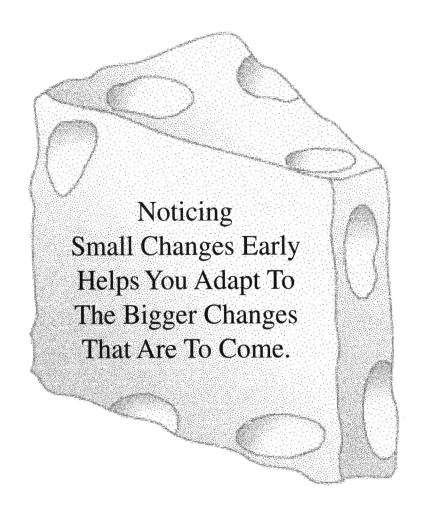

Noticing
Small Changes Early
Helps You Adapt To
The Bigger Changes
That Are To Come.

By now, Haw had let go of the past and was adapting to the present.

He continued on through the maze with greater strength and speed. And before long, it happened.

When it seemed like he had been in the maze forever, his journey—or at least this part of his journey—ended quickly and happily.

Haw proceeded along a corridor that was new to him, rounded a corner, and found New Cheese at Cheese Station N!

When he went inside, he was startled by what he saw. Piled high everywhere was the greatest supply of Cheese he had ever seen. He didn't recognize all that he saw, as some kinds of Cheese were new to him.

Then he wondered for a moment whether it was real or just his imagination, until he saw his old friends Sniff and Scurry.

Sniff welcomed Haw with a nod of his head, and Scurry waved his paw. Their fat little bellies showed that they had been here for some time.

Haw quickly said his hellos and soon took bites of every one of his favorite Cheeses. He pulled off his shoes, tied the laces together, and hung them around his neck in case he needed them again. Sniff and Scurry laughed. They nodded their heads in admiration. Then Haw jumped into the New Cheese. When he had eaten his fill, he lifted a piece of fresh Cheese and made a toast. "Hooray for Change!"

As Haw enjoyed the New Cheese, he reflected on what he had learned.

He realized that when he had been afraid to change he had been holding on to the illusion of Old Cheese that was no longer there.

So what was it that made him change? Was it the fear of starving to death? Haw smiled as he thought it certainly helped.

Then he laughed and realized that he had started to change as soon as he had learned to laugh at himself and at what he had been doing wrong. He realized the fastest way to change is to laugh at your own folly—then you can let go and quickly move on.

He knew he had learned something useful about moving on from his mice friends, Sniff and Scurry. They kept life simple. They didn't overanalyze or overcomplicate things. When the situation changed and the Cheese had been moved, they changed and moved with the Cheese. He would remember that.

Haw had also used his wonderful brain to do what littlepeople do better than mice.

He envisioned himself—in realistic detail—finding something better—much better.

He reflected on the mistakes he had made in the past and used them to plan for his future. He knew that you could learn to deal with change:

You could be more aware of the need to keep things simple, be flexible, and move quickly.

You did not need to overcomplicate matters or confuse yourself with fearful beliefs.

You could notice when the little changes began so that you would be better prepared for the big change that might be coming.

He knew he needed to adapt faster, for if you do not adapt in time, you might as well not adapt at all.

He had to admit that the biggest inhibitor to change lies within yourself, and that nothing gets better until *you* change.

Perhaps most importantly, he realized that there is always New Cheese out there whether you recognize it at the time, or not. And that you are rewarded with it when you go past your fear and enjoy the adventure.

He knew some fear should be respected, as it can keep you out of real danger. But he realized most of his fears were irrational and had kept him from changing when he needed to.

He didn't like it at the time, but he knew that the change had turned out to be a blessing in disguise as it led him to find better Cheese.

He had even found a better part of himself.

As Haw recalled what he had learned, he thought about his friend Hem. He wondered if Hem had read any of the sayings Haw had written on the wall at Cheese Station C and throughout the Maze.

Had Hem ever decided to let go and move on? Had he ever entered the Maze and discovered what could make his life better?

Or was Hem still hemmed in because he would not change?

Haw thought about going back again to Cheese Station C to see if he could find Hem—assuming that Haw could find his way back there. If he found Hem, he thought he might be able to show him how to get out of his predicament. But Haw realized that he had already tried to get his friend to change.

Hem had to find his own way, beyond his comforts and past his fears. No one else could do it for him, or talk him into it. He somehow had to see the advantage of changing himself.

Haw knew he had left a trail for Hem and that he could find his way, if he could just read The Handwriting On The Wall.

He went over and wrote down a summary of what he had learned on the largest wall of Cheese Station N. He drew a large piece of cheese around all the insights he had become aware of, and smiled as he looked at what he had learned:

THE HANDWRITING ON THE WALL

Change Happens
They Keep Moving The Cheese

Anticipate Change
Get Ready For The Cheese To Move

Monitor Change
Smell The Cheese Often So You
Know When It Is Getting Old

Adapt To Change Quickly
The Quicker You Let Go Of Old Cheese,
The Sooner You Can Enjoy New Cheese

Change
Move With The Cheese

Enjoy Change!
Savor The Adventure And
Enjoy The Taste Of New Cheese!

Be Ready To Change Quickly And Enjoy It Again & Again
They Keep Moving The Cheese

Haw realized how far he had come since he had been with Hem in Cheese Station C, but knew it would be easy for him to slip back if he got too comfortable. So each day he inspected Cheese Station N to see what the condition of his Cheese was. He was going to do whatever he could to avoid being surprised by unexpected change.

While Haw still had a great supply of Cheese, he often went out into the maze and explored new areas to stay in touch with what was happening around him. He knew it was safer to be aware of his real choices than to isolate himself in his comfort zone.

Then, Haw heard what he thought was the sound of movement out in the maze. As the noise grew louder, he realized that someone was coming.

Could it be that Hem was arriving? Was he about to turn the corner?

Haw said a little prayer and hoped—as he had many times before—that maybe, at last, his friend was finally able to . . .

Move With
The Cheese
And Enjoy It!

the end . . .
or is it a new beginning?

A Discussion
Later That Same Day

When Michael finished telling the story, he looked around the room and saw his former classmates smiling at him.

Several thanked him and said they got a good deal out of the story.

Nathan asked the group, "What would you think of getting together later and maybe discussing it?"

Most of them said they would like to talk about it, and so they arranged to meet later for a drink before dinner.

That evening, as they gathered in a hotel lounge, they began to kid each other about finding their "Cheese" and seeing themselves in the maze.

Then Angela asked the group good-naturedly, "So, who were you in the story? Sniff, Scurry, Hem or Haw?"

Carlos answered, "Well, I was thinking about that this afternoon. I clearly remember a time before I had my sporting goods business, when I had a rough encounter with change.

"I wasn't Sniff—I didn't sniff out the situation and see the change early. And I certainly wasn't Scurry—I didn't go into action immediately.

"I was more like Hem, who wanted to stay in familiar territory. The truth is, I didn't want to deal with the change. I didn't even want to see it."

Michael, who felt like no time had passed since he and Carlos were close friends in school, asked, "What are we talking about here, buddy?"

Carlos said, "An unexpected change of jobs."

Michael laughed. "You were fired?"

"Well let's just say I didn't want to go out looking for New Cheese. I thought I had a good reason why change shouldn't happen to me. So, I was pretty upset at the time."

Some of their former classmates who had been quiet in the beginning felt more comfortable now and spoke up, including Frank, who had gone into the military.

"Hem reminds me of a friend of mine," Frank said. "His department was closing down, but he didn't want to see it. They kept relocating his people. We all tried to talk to him about the many other opportunities that existed in the company for those who wanted to be flexible, but he didn't think he had to change. He was the only one who was surprised when his department closed. Now he's having a hard time adjusting to the change he didn't think should happen."

Jessica said, "I didn't think it should happen to me either, but my 'Cheese' has been moved more than once, especially in my personal life, but we can get to that later."

Many in the group laughed, except Nathan.

"Maybe that's the whole point," Nathan said. "Change happens to all of us."

He added, "I wish my family had heard the Cheese story before this. Unfortunately we didn't want to see the changes coming in our business, and now it's too late—we're having to close many of our stores."

That surprised many in the group, because they thought Nathan was lucky to be in a secure business he could depend on, year after year.

"What happened?" Jessica wanted to know.

"Our chain of small stores suddenly became old fashioned when the mega-store came to town with its huge inventory and low prices. We just couldn't compete with that.

"I can see now that instead of being like Sniff and Scurry, we were like Hem. We stayed where we were and didn't change. We tried to ignore what was happening and now we are in trouble. We could have taken a couple of lessons from Haw—because we certainly couldn't laugh at ourselves and change what we were doing."

Laura, who had become a successful business-woman, had been listening, but had said very little until now. "I thought about the story this afternoon too," she said. "I wondered how I could be more like Haw and see what I'm doing wrong, laugh at myself, change, and do better."

She said, "I'm curious. How many here are afraid of change?" No one responded, so she suggested, "How about a show of hands?"

Only one hand went up. "Well, it looks like we've got one honest person in our group!" she said. And then continued, "Maybe you'll like this next question better. How many here think other people are afraid of change?" Practically everyone raised their hands. Then they all started laughing.

"What does *that* tell us?"

"Denial," Nathan answered.

"Sure," Michael admitted, "sometimes we're not even aware that we're afraid. I know I wasn't. When I first heard the story, I loved the question, 'What would you do if you weren't afraid?'"

Then Jessica added, "Well, what I got from the story is that change is happening everywhere and that I will do better when I can adjust to it quickly.

"I remember years ago when our company was selling our encyclopedia as a set of more than twenty books. One person tried to tell us that we should put our whole encyclopedia on a single computer disk and sell it for a fraction of the cost. It would be easier to update, would cost us so much less to manufacture, and so many more people could afford it. But we all resisted."

"Why did you resist?" Nathan asked.

"Because, we believed then that the backbone of our business was our large sales force, who called on people door-to-door. Keeping our sales force depended on the big commissions they earned from the high price of our product. We had been doing this successfully for a long time and thought it would go on forever."

Laura said, "Maybe that's what it meant in the story about Hem and Haw's arrogance of success. They didn't notice they needed to change what had once been working."

Nathan said, "So you thought your old Cheese was your only Cheese."

"Yes, and we wanted to hang on to it.

"When I think back on what happened to us, I see that it's not just that they 'moved the Cheese,' but that the 'Cheese' has a life of its own and eventually runs out.

"Anyway, we didn't change. But a competitor did and our sales fell badly. We've been going through a difficult time. Now, another big technological change is happening in the industry and no one at the company seems to want to deal with it. It doesn't look good. I think I could be out of a job soon."

"It's MAZE time!" Carlos called out. Everyone laughed, including Jessica.

Carlos turned to Jessica and said, "It's good that you can laugh at yourself."

Frank offered, "That's what *I* got out of the story. I tend to take myself too seriously. I noticed how Haw changed when he could finally laugh at himself and at what he was doing. No wonder he was called Haw."

The group groaned at the obvious play on words.

Angela asked, "Do you think that Hem ever changed and found New Cheese?"

Elaine said, "I think he did."

"I don't," Cory said. "Some people never change and they pay a price for it. I see people like Hem in my medical practice. They feel entitled to their 'Cheese.' They feel like victims when it's taken away and blame others. They get sicker than people who let go and move on."

Then Nathan said quietly, as though he was talking to himself, "I guess the question is, 'What do we need to let go of and what do we need to move on to?'"

No one said anything for a while.

"I must admit," Nathan said, "I saw what was happening with stores like ours in other parts of the country, but I hoped it wouldn't affect us. I guess it's a lot better to initiate change while you can than it is to try to react and adjust to it. Maybe we should move our own Cheese."

"What do you mean?" Frank asked.

Nathan answered, "I can't help but wonder where we would be today if we had sold the real estate under all our old stores and built one great modern store to compete with the best of them."

Laura said, "Maybe that's what Haw meant when he wrote on the wall 'Savor the adventure and move with the Cheese.'"

Frank said, "I think some things shouldn't change. For example, I want to hold on to my basic values. But I realize now that I would be better off if I had moved with the 'Cheese' a lot sooner in my life."

"Well, Michael, it was a nice little story," Richard, the class skeptic, said, "but how did you actually put it into use in your company?"

The group didn't know it yet, but Richard was experiencing some changes himself. Recently separated from his wife, he was now trying to balance his career with raising his teenagers.

Michael replied, "You know, I thought my job was just to manage the daily problems as they came up when what I should have been doing was looking ahead and paying attention to where we were going.

"And boy did I manage those problems—twenty-four hours a day. I wasn't a lot of fun to be around. I was in a rat race and I couldn't get out."

Laura said, "So you were managing when you needed to be leading."

"Exactly," Michael said. "Then when I heard the story of *Who Moved My Cheese?*, I realized my job was to paint a picture of 'New Cheese' that we would all want to pursue, so we could enjoy changing and succeeding, whether it was at work or in life.

Nathan asked, "What did you do at work?"

"Well, when I asked people in our company who they were in the Story, I saw we had every one of the four characters in our organization. I came to see the Sniffs, Scurrys, Hems, and Haws each needed to be treated differently.

"Our Sniffs could sniff out changes in the marketplace, so they helped us update our corporate vision. They were encouraged to identify how the changes could result in new products and services our customers would want. The Sniffs loved it and told us they enjoyed working in a place that recognized change and adapted in time.

"Our Scurrys liked to get things done, so they were encouraged to take actions, based on the new corporate vision. They just needed to be monitored so they didn't scurry off in the wrong direction. They were then rewarded for actions that brought us New Cheese. They liked working in a company that valued action and results."

"What about the Hems and Haws?" Angela asked.

"Unfortunately, the Hems were the anchors that slowed us down," Michael answered. "They were either too comfortable or too afraid to change. Some of our Hems changed only when they saw the sensible vision we painted that showed them how changing would work to their advantage.

"Our Hems told us they wanted to work in a place that was safe, so the changes needed to make sense to them and increase their sense of security. When they realized the real danger of not changing, some of them changed and did well. The vision helped us turn many of our Hems into Haws."

"What did you do with the Hems who didn't change?" Frank wanted to know.

"We had to let them go," Michael said sadly. "We wanted to keep all our employees, but we knew if our business didn't change quickly enough, we would all be in trouble."

Then he said, "The good news is that while our Haws were initially hesitant, they were open-minded enough to learn something new, act differently, and adapt in time to help us succeed.

"They came to expect change and actively look for it. Because they understood human nature, they helped us paint a realistic vision of New Cheese that made good sense to practically everyone.

"They told us they wanted to work in an organization that gave people the confidence and tools to change. And they helped us keep our sense of humor as we went after our New Cheese."

Richard commented, "You got all that from a little story?"

Michael smiled. "It wasn't the story, but what we *did* differently based on what we took from it."

Angela admitted, "I'm a little bit like Hem, so for me, the most powerful part of the story was when Haw laughed at his fear and went on to paint a picture in his mind, where he saw himself enjoying 'New Cheese.' It made going into the Maze less fearful and more enjoyable. And he eventually got a better deal. That's what I want to do more often."

Frank grinned. "So even Hems can sometimes see the advantage of changing."

Carlos laughed. "Like the advantage of keeping their jobs."

Angela added, "Or even getting a good raise."

Richard, who had been frowning during the discussion, said, "My manager's been telling me our company needs to change. I think what she's really telling me is that *I* need to, but I haven't wanted to hear it. I guess I never really knew what the 'New Cheese' was that she was trying to move us to. Or how I could gain from it."

A slight smile crossed Richard's face as he said, "I must admit I like this idea of seeing 'New Cheese' and imagining yourself enjoying it. It lightens everything up. When you see how it can make things better, you get more interested in making the change happen.

"Maybe I could use this in my personal life," he added. "My children seem to think that nothing in their lives should ever change. I guess they're acting like Hem—they're angry. They're probably afraid of what the future holds. Maybe I haven't painted a realistic picture of 'New Cheese' for them. Probably because I don't see it myself."

The group was quiet as several people thought about their own lives.

"Well," Jessica said, "most people here are talking about jobs, but as I listened to the story, I thought about my personal life. I think my current relationship is 'Old Cheese' that has some pretty serious mold on it."

Cory laughed in agreement. "Me too. I probably need to let go of a bad relationship."

Angela countered, "Or, perhaps the 'Old Cheese' is just old behavior. What we really need to let go of is the behavior that is the cause of our bad relationship. And then move on to a better way of thinking and acting."

"Ouch!" Cory reacted. "Good point. The New Cheese is a new relationship with the same person."

Richard said, "I'm beginning to think there is more to this than I thought. I like the idea of letting go of old behavior instead of letting go of the relationship. Repeating the same behavior will just get you the same results.

"As far as work goes, maybe instead of changing jobs I should be changing the way I am *doing* my job. I'd probably have a better position by now if I did."

Then Becky, who lived in another city but had returned for the reunion, said, "As I was listening to the story and to everyone's comments here, I've had to laugh at myself. I've been like Hem for so long, hemming and hawing and afraid of change. I didn't realize how many other people did this as well. I'm afraid I've passed it on to my children without even knowing it.

"As I think about it, I realize change really can lead you to a new and better place, although you're afraid it won't at the time.

"I remember a time when our son was a sophomore in high school. My husband's job required us to move from Illinois to Vermont and our son was upset because he had to leave his friends. He was a star swimmer and the high school in Vermont had no swim team. So, he was angry with us for making him move.

"As it turned out, he fell in love with the Vermont mountains, took up skiing, skied on his college team and now lives happily in Colorado.

"If we had all enjoyed this Cheese story together, over a cup of hot chocolate, we could have saved our family a lot of stress."

Jessica said, "I'm going home to tell my family this story. I'll ask my children who they think I am—Sniff, Scurry, Hem or Haw—and who they feel they are. We could talk about what we feel our family's Old Cheese is and what the New Cheese could be."

"That's a good idea," Richard said, surprising everyone—even himself.

Frank then commented, "I think I'm going to be more like Haw and move with the Cheese and enjoy it! And I'm going to pass this story along to my friends who are worried about leaving the military and what the change might mean to them. It could lead to some interesting discussions."

Michael said, "Well, that's how we improved our business. We had several discussions about what we got from the Cheese story and how we could apply it to our own situation.

"It was great because we had language that was fun for us to use to talk about how we were dealing with change. It was very effective, especially as it spread deeper into the company."

Nathan asked, "What do you mean by 'deeper'?"

"Well, the further we went into our organization, the more people we found who felt they had less power. They were understandably more afraid of what the change imposed from above might do to them. So they resisted change.

"In short, a change imposed is a change opposed.

"But when the Cheese Story was shared with literally everyone in our organization, it helped us change the way we looked at change. It helped everyone laugh, or at least smile, at their old fears and want to move on.

"I only wished I'd heard the Cheese story sooner," Michael added.

"How come?" Carlos asked.

"Because by the time we got around to addressing the changes, our business had already fallen off so badly that we had to let people go, as I said earlier, including some good friends. It was hard on all of us. However, those who stayed and most of those who left said the Cheese story helped them see things differently and cope better.

"Those who had to go out and look for a new job said it was hard at first but recalling the story was a great help to them."

Angela asked, "What helped them most?"

Michael replied, "After they got past their fear, they told me the best thing was realizing that there was New Cheese out there just waiting to be found!

"They said holding a picture of New Cheese in their minds—seeing themselves doing well in a new job—made them feel better, and helped them *do* better in job interviews. Several got better jobs."

Laura asked, "What about the people who remained in your company?"

"Well," Michael said, "instead of complaining about the changes that were happening, people now said, 'They just moved our Cheese. Let's look for the New Cheese.' It saved a lot of time and reduced stress.

"Before long, the people who had been resisting saw the advantage of changing. They even helped bring about change."

Cory said, "Why do you think they changed?"

"They changed after the peer pressure in our company changed."

He asked, "What happens in most organizations you've been in when a change is announced by top management? Do most people say the change is a great idea or a bad idea?"

"A bad idea," Frank answered.

"Yes," Michael agreed. "Why?"

Carlos said, "Because people want things to stay the same and they think the change will be bad for them. When one person says the change is a bad idea, others say the same."

"Yes, they may not really feel that way," Michael said, "but they agree in order to fit in. That's the sort of peer pressure that fights change in any organization."

Becky asked, "So how were things different after people heard the Cheese story?"

Michael said simply, "The peer pressure changed because no one wanted to look like Hem!"

Everyone laughed.

"They wanted to sniff out the changes ahead of time and scurry into action, rather than get hemmed in and be left behind."

Nathan said, "That's a good point. No one in our company would want to look like Hem. They might even change. Why didn't you tell us this story at our last reunion? This could work."

Michael said, "It does work.

"It works best, of course, when everyone in your organization knows the story—whether it is in a large corporation, a small business or your family—because an organization can only change when enough people in it change."

Then he offered one last thought. "When we saw how well it worked for us, we passed the story along to people we wanted to do business with, knowing they were also dealing with change. We suggested we might be their 'New Cheese,' that is, better partners for them to succeed with. It led to new business."

That gave Jessica several ideas and reminded her that she had some early sales calls in the morning. She looked at her watch and said, "Well, it's time for me to leave this Cheese Station and find some New Cheese."

The group laughed and began saying their good-byes. Many of them wanted to continue the conversation but needed to leave. As they left, they thanked Michael again.

He said, "I'm very glad you found the story so useful, and I hope that you will have the opportunity to share it with others soon."

the end

Share It With Others

About the Author

Spencer Johnson, M.D., is an internationally respected thought leader, speaker, and author whose insights have helped millions of people discover simple truths they can use to have healthier lives with more success and less stress.

He has often been referred to as the best there is at taking complex subjects and presenting simple solutions that work.

He is the author and co-author of the #1 bestselling books *Who Moved My Cheese?,* an amazing way to deal with change; and *The One Minute Manager®,* written with legendary management consultant Kenneth Blanchard, Ph.D., which continues to appear on Business Bestseller Lists and has become the world's most popular management method.

He has written many other bestsellers, including *The Precious Present,* a perennial gift favorite; *Yes or No,* a guide to better decisions; *ValueTales®,* the popular children's books; and five other books in the *One Minute®* series: *The One Minute $ales Person, The One Minute Mother, The One Minute Father, The One Minute Teacher,* and *One Minute For Yourself.*

His education includes a B.A. in psychology from the University of Southern California, an M.D. degree from the Royal College of Surgeons, and medical clerkships at Harvard Medical School and The Mayo Clinic.

Dr. Johnson was Medical Director of Communications for Medtronic, the inventors of cardiac pacemakers; Research Physician at The Institute for Inter-Disciplinary Studies, a think tank; and Consultant to the Center for the Study of the Person, and the School of Medicine, University of California.

His books have been featured often in the media, including CNN, The Today Show, Larry King Show, *Time Magazine, Business Week, The New York Times, Wall Street Journal, USA Today,* Associated Press, and United Press International.

Spencer Johnson's books are available worldwide in twenty-six languages.